Ethics and Spirituality

Ethics and Spirituality

An Activity Book

Roy H. May Jr.

WIPF & STOCK · Eugene, Oregon

ETHICS AND SPIRITUALITY
An Activity Book

Copyright © 2012 Roy H. May Jr.. All rights reserved. Except for brief quotations in critical publications or reviews, no part of this book may be reproduced in any manner without prior written permission from the publisher. Write: Permissions, Wipf and Stock Publishers, 199 W. 8th Ave., Suite 3, Eugene, OR 97401.

Wipf & Stock
An Imprint of Wipf and Stock Publishers
199 W. 8th Ave., Suite 3
Eugene, OR 97401
www.wipfandstock.com

ISBN 13: 978-1-62032-253-6
Manufactured in the U.S.A.

Original title: *Ética y espiritualidad, pastoral de la espiritualidad* 17. Curso de Educación Pastoral (CEPA). San José, Costa Rica: Universidad Bíblica Latinoamericana. Translation and revisions by Roy H. May Jr.

Scripture quotations, unless otherwise indicated, are from the New Revised Standard Version (NRSV), Copyright©1989, Division of Christian Education of the National Council of the Churches of Christ in the United States of America. Used by Permission. All rights reserved. Scripture quotations marked (GNT) are from the Good News Translation in Today's English Version—Second Edition Copyright©1992 American Bible Society. Used by Permission. Scripture quotations marked (NLT) are taken from the Holy Bible New Living Translation, Copyright©1996, 2004, 2007 by Tyndale House Publishers, Inc., Carol Stream, Illinois 60188. All rights reserved.

The photograph in Practice 20 is by Armando Del Vecchio / UV Studio. Reproduced by permission.

Contents

Preface vii
Introduction xi

1. Living According to the Spirit 1
    Step 1 Spirituality: Person and Community
    Step 2 Ethics and Spirituality for Life

2. Ethical Problems and Spiritual Life 10
    Step 1 Who Is My Neighbor?
    Step 2 Spirituality and Community
    Step 3 Spiritual and Ethical Formation

3. Ethical and Spiritual Values 20
    Step 1 Sin, World, and Flesh
    Step 2 Bible, Church, and Values
    Step 3 Values for a Spirituality for Life

4. Biblical and Spiritual Ethics 34
    Step 1 Social Justice and the Prophetic Tradition
    Step 2 Spirituality in Action
    Step 3 Jesus and the Gospel Traditions

5. Moral Discernment and Spirituality for Convivial Living 43
    Step 1 Moral Reasoning
    Step 2 How to Make a Moral Decision
    Step 3 Living Responsibly

6. Moral Imagination 54
    Step 1 Moral Situations

Bibliography 59

Preface

ROY H. MAY JR. offers the reader a highly worthwhile and stimulating read, a thinking and seeking person's book. He calls it "an activity book" and indeed it is just that. He makes spirituality and ethics a lively invitation and challenge led by the Holy Spirit.

What distinguishes this book from many others who traverse similar terrain in the field of ethics and spirituality are the distinct and unique connections the author is able to make. I will mention just two of these special features.

Roy May connects the Anglo and Latin worlds based on his experience and training in both cultures over the years. This present work in its original edition has already achieved respect and wide use in Latin America based on his long and distinguished ministry as a professor at the Latin American Biblical University in San José, Costa Rica. Specifically, the book has a history in Spanish, having been used as a study book for lay education through the Council of Latin American Churches. Professor May has now done some revising to address the U. S. context as well.

His thinking and writing are deeply influenced by a Latin American sense of spirituality shared through community responsibility. Outcroppings of Latin American liberation theology based on social justice abound to inform the reader. Examples include terms as "preferential option for the poor;" *convivencia* or living with, similar to the English terms conviviality or convivial; and references to the murdered Jesuit, Fr. Ignacio Ellacuría and to his Jesuit colleague, Fr. Jon Sobrino.

At the same time May's writing connects with current issues in the United States where he received his early training for ministry through the United Methodist Church and where he maintains many contacts. His biblical examples include the parable of the Good Samaritan (Luke 10:29–37) and Jesus's proclamation of his ministry's purpose in Luke 4:16–21. I mention these because in both instances May draws the texts into our own U. S. culture by asking the question, "Who are those in the

Preface

Good Samaritan narrative in our U. S. culture?" and similarly, "Who are the blind and the oppressed today in the U. S. mentioned by Jesus in his hometown synagogue?" It is May's ability to connect the biblical past with the present in both Latin and U. S. societies that makes for lively reading and learning.

A second connection May holds before us is the close relationship between the pastoral and the prophetic in considering and living out our responses to spiritually-based ethics or ethics-based spirituality. Undergirding May's whole work is the reality that the pastoral and the prophetic ministry of the church is one seamless garment of God's love for the world and its people.

Building up community is the responsibility of pastoral theology and practice. But because this necessitates facing and grappling with inconvenient power issues, there is automatically a prophetic function calling for social justice. One way in which May addresses the connection of the pastoral and the prophetic is his mention of Bonhoeffer's allusion to cheap and costly grace. Likewise, cheap love is love without justice whereas costly love is based on justice.

As insisted in the Micah 6 text lifted up by May, justice and mercy, or love, need each other as basic to faith. Although not mentioned in this particular writing, Jesus makes exactly the same point in Matthew 23:23 where he upbraids the religious establishment for neglecting the weightier matters of the law, namely, justice, mercy, and faith (RSV). This sacred trilogy, as I like to call it, is an actively named yet sometimes silent theme coursing through the veins of May's work.

May's book concludes with a thoughtful and helpful section on moral discernment and reasoning and how to make a moral decision. I'll leave it to the reader to test these out, but I found his crafting of decisions based on rules, consequences, and circumstances, suggesting the strengths and weaknesses of each, to be icing on an already rich cake of ethics and spirituality.

Throughout the book May posits questions for the reader to address, preferably in a group setting. He provides guidelines for spiritually-based ethical decisions but not concrete answers. He respects and encourages the reader's ability to reflect and develop moral imagination and arrive at one's own responses. And how many authors writing on spiritual and ethical issues have encouraged us to have fun as we deliberate on these critical issues?

Preface

I believe this latest work from Roy May reveals the fruit of his thinking and doing at its best. The Salvadoran Jesuit Jon Sobrino has said, "If you in this country keep working in whatever ways you can for the crucified peoples of the earth—in the United States, in El Salvador, wherever—your lives will have more meaning; your faith will be more Christian; your hope will be stronger." A reading of May's *Ethics and Spirituality: An Activity Book* will lead you towards Sobrino's claim.

—William K. McElvaney

Preface

Objectives:

1. To understand ethics as spirituality.
2. To provide theoretical tools and practices for doing ethics and living spiritually.
3. To clarify one's own manner of approaching ethical questions, founding moral values, and theological positions that undergird ethics and spirituality.

Introduction

Living Spiritually

SAINT PAUL DECLARES, "LIVE by the Spirit" (Gal 5:16). This means that our way of living, whether it be through our personal or our social behavior, ought to be "led" (Gal 5:18) or "guided" by the Holy Spirit (Gal 5:25). This is "spirituality" for it is the Holy Spirit that illuminates the pathways of life and helps us understand how to live meaningfully. Theologian Lewis Mudge tells us that:

> spirituality . . . mean[s] the depth dimension of daily existence cultivated by both meditative and moral practices. The meditative and the moral, indeed, cannot be separated. They are part of one whole cloth. Spirituality can now mean the whole shape, the shared fabric, of human lives in God.[1]

So "spirituality" means to walk the pathways of life discerning where the Holy Spirit wishes to lead us.

Spirituality implies a whole style of life. And given that our life in this world is founded on, and necessarily shaped by, relationships with other persons, with God, with ourselves, and even with other living creatures, spirituality has to do with the way we live out these multiple relationships. It is a whole way of living and relating in the world: "For the whole law is summed up in a single commandment, 'You shall love your neighbor as yourself'" (Gal 5:14). If this is spirituality, it is also ethics. As the great theologian of the twentieth century, Paul Tillich (1886–1965), reminded us, "And this is the meaning of ethics: the expression of the ways in which love embodies itself and life is maintained and saved."[2] Thus Saint Paul calls on the Galatians to "live by the Spirit."

---

1. Mudge, *Church as Moral Community*, 83.
2. Tillich, *Morality and Beyond*, 95.

Introduction

In the early tradition of the Church, the Holy Spirit unites humanity (Eph 4:16). It energizes it and leads it toward righteousness, justice, solidarity, and community. It signals dialogue and communication that make community life possible. Several years ago a group of Christians concerned about the environment wrote this about the Holy Spirit:

> The Spirit is the giver and sustainer of life. All that fosters life, such as justice, solidarity and love, and all that defends life, such as the evangelical commitment to stand with the poor, the struggle against racism and casteism, and the pledge to reduce armaments and violence, concretely signifies living according to the Spirit . . . Even more, to live according to the Spirit is to capture its presence in all Creation.[3]

Do you believe they were talking about the Holy Spirit? Why?

The Holy Spirit is the interpretation or theological name we give to our capacity to discern and to imagine creatively and qualitatively new relationships that maintain and save life. And by interpreting theologically this capacity, we place it in the dimension of ultimacy—as a manifestation of Ultimate Reality, as Tillich would say—and therefore of ultimate concern and importance.

In this sense, the Holy Spirit moves us toward encountering and committing ourselves to our neighbors. Spirituality is born in this human encounter and commitment, when God—Ultimate Reality—is found in the face of the other person. Spirituality, then, is based on compassion and empathy. Compassion signifies pity for and commitment to persons in need. Empathy points to the capacity to enter into solidarity with persons in need. It signifies putting oneself in the shoes of the other, and feeling and thinking with her or him. It makes their joys and pains our own. Being led by the Spirit leads to one's neighbors.

Spirituality and Responsibility

Far from separating us from the world, spirituality leads us *toward* the world. Far from evading responsibility, it means *taking* responsibility—for knowing what's going on around us and responding appropriately. So spirituality doesn't mean participating in more worship services or spending more time in prayer than other people. It doesn't mean studying

3. Grandberg-Michelson, *Redeeming Creation*, 72.

Introduction

the Bible more than others. Nor does it mean having extraordinary mystical or ecstatic experiences. A person might indeed live a spirituality that includes all of this, but one isn't spiritual because of it. Take a moment to read Isaiah 58:1–14. What does "spirituality" mean for the prophet? He's very direct: What makes one spiritual is the way we relate to and care for those around us: other people and the natural world. So spirituality, as theologians Karen Lebacqz and Joseph Driskill say, "requires that attention to the inner life of search be placed in the context of concerns about social, historical, environmental, structural, institutional, and interpersonal issues."[4]

Of course there isn't a single expression of spirituality. Lebacqz and Driskill remind us that it has "many faces."[5] Saint Paul was very clear when he wrote the Corinthians, "Now there are varieties of gifts . . . and there are varieties of services . . . and there are varieties of activities" (1 Cor 12:4–6). What is fundamental is love (1 Cor 13:13). Therefore, spirituality signifies living in such a way that others recognize the presence of God in one's life. "If we live by the Spirit, let us also be guided by the Spirit" (Gal 5:25). Spirituality resounds in our lifestyles and our way of relating to others, in short, in our ethics.

How to Use this Activity Book

So with this introduction, I invite you to explore more deeply about living by the Spirit. I hope this book will help you. Its various themes are organized into six short "conversations." In a good conversation, each person contributes ideas and other thoughts that are helpful and useful. There is dialogue. Each "conversation" contributes what I think will be helpful as you think about ethics and spirituality. But I want you to respond so that this isn't just one way. That wouldn't be a conversation. So these conversations, in turn, are divided into "steps." I call them steps because I think of this activity book as a kind of journey or *caminata* in Spanish—a good walk or trek—where each step takes you along a path toward understanding. Interspersed throughout are "practices" or activities related to the various themes for you to do both individually and with a group. I hope you'll do this activity book with a group. Spirituality and ethics are really

---

4. Lebacqz and Driskill, *Ethics and Spiritual Care*, 33.
5. Ibid., 19.

Introduction

communal, something we do together. This is working *en conjunto*, sharing, arguing, proposing, but coming together as one body, not necessarily in agreement but respecting one another anyway. We need each other for the journey. So studying *en conjunto* will enrich your journey into ethics and spirituality.

Finally, I close by inviting you to exercise your moral imagination through focusing on a series of moral situations for you to deal with. This part is really up to you. It's your "conversation." I have my own answers for these cases, but I haven't written that part. Really, there aren't any "right" or "wrong" answers. So it's up to you and your group to discern how you believe one should respond. I hope you'll enjoy doing this. Ethics and spirituality should be about joyous and convivial living. So have fun as you explore the ideas I'm sharing with you.

Conversation 1

Living According to the Spirit

Step 1
Spirituality: Person and Community

Practice 1

For personal reflection

1. What does spirituality mean for you? What are some characteristics of life led by the Spirit?
2. In the practices of your own church, what are some of the things that contribute toward your living a spiritual life?

For group reflection

1. Share and compare your ideas about spirituality.
2. Find some biblical texts about spirituality. How are they different, how are they alike?

You undoubtedly found that life led by the Spirit has many definitions and aspects.

So, where does the Spirit guide you? As I have said, according to Saint Paul the Holy Spirit leads us towards committing ourselves lovingly to others, our "neighbors." Robin Meyer, a United Church of Christ pastor in Oklahoma, reminds us, powerfully so, that "it is *relationships*, not transactions, that hold the key to human happiness. We are as we

Ethics and Spirituality

relate—not as we possess, control, believe, or conquer."[1] This relational or communitarian dimension conditions our basic values and commitments. Spirituality too often is understood as an individualistic, even solitary experience. For Saint Paul, however, being led by the Spirit occurs through our relationships and consequent community life. Indeed, for the Apostle, spirituality is fundamentally about living together in community.

To describe this, Saint Paul often uses the Greek word *koinonia*. We can find the word in several places: Romans 6:6, "with him"; 15:26–27, "to share"; 1 Corinthians 1:9, "fellowship"; 9:23, "share"; 10:16–17, "sharing, we all partake"; 2 Corinthians 7:3, "together"; 8:4, "sharing"; 8:23, "partner, co-worker"; 9:13, "sharing"; Galatians 2:9, "fellowship"; 6:6, "share"; and Philemon 17, "partner." *Koinonia* also is used in Acts 2:42, 44, and 4:32, where it means fellowship and to have something in common or sharing together. The Johannine literature, especially 1 John, express very similar ideas with the word *agape* or love expressed in a deeply caring and serving way.

Koinonia means communion, community, collaboration, participation, solidarity, sharing, and unity. It also signifies partner and participant. So *koinonia* signals life-in-community or life together: people's living relationships with others. But *koinonia* as life-in-community points especially to the *quality* of these relations as characterized by love and joy. The Spanish word *convivencia*—literally "living with"—expresses well the idea of *koinonia*. *Convivencia* (similar to the little used English noun "conviviality" or its adjective form "convivial") means living together under the same roof, that is, together in the same house. Especially in the Andean region of South America, the word often is used for a friendly get-together, such as a party or an informal meal among friends. It connotes joy, friendship, and mutual commitment. My friend Diego Irarrázaval, a Chilean priest who worked for many years in the high Andes of southern Peru, underlines this. From his pastoral experience he says that we "live together" in order "to live well." He roots ethics in "merriment" because "Jesus's spirituality was rooted in joy." For Diego, "to live together," as for the Andean people, "culminates in *fiesta*" or "joyful *convivencia*."[2] This is the quality of life that *koinonia* evokes: convivial life.

---

1. Meyer, *Saving Jesus from the Church*, 203–4. Chapter 10 is devoted to religion as relationships.

2. Irarrázaval, *Gozar la ética*, 14, 107, 108.

Saint Paul underscores this communitarian or "convivial" dimension of the Christian life through the image of the body:

> For just as the body is one and has many members, and all the members of the body, though many, are one body, so it is with Christ. For in the one Spirit we are all baptized into one body— Jews or Greeks, slaves or free—and we were all made to drink of the one Spirit. (1 Cor 12:12–13)

What makes life-in-community possible?

Saint Paul tells us that life-in-community is possible through the Holy Spirit. The Holy Spirit makes us one body. Spirituality, then, refers to living in such a way as to foment life together, convivial life.

We can envision such a life as having four, overlapping dimensions:

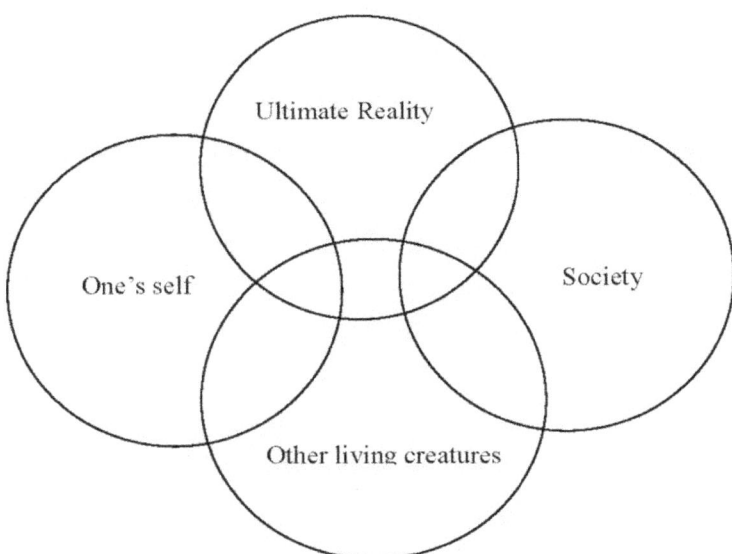

As you can see in the diagram, every person is integrally related to him or herself, to other people, to other living creatures and the natural order, and all are rooted in God as Ultimate Reality.

Ethics and Spirituality

Relations with God

Here I am thinking of God as Ultimate Reality, the very basis of all existence—the "ground of being" as Tillich often said. This is the Reality that forms life out of relationships and thus makes all relationships possible. It founds existence and its many expressions. In this Ultimate Reality "we live and move and have our being" (Acts 17:28). Thus God is also Ultimate Creativity or Creativity itself, to follow the idea of the late theologian Gordon Kaufman.[3] As people, we are an inseparable part of these Creative relationships. Indeed, we manifest them through our own many creative relationships. Creativity is the Ultimate Reality that makes existence possible and therefore is the basis of all relationships. "God" is the name we give to this creative, ultimate reality that grounds and makes possible our very existence. In this sense, God is present in all dimensions of life. We cannot escape relating to God, even when we don't consciously do so.

Relations with one's self

Every individual person is deeply related to his or her own person. As an individual, I can know myself, my thoughts and ideas, likes and dislikes, feelings and motives. I am conscious of my own being *vis-à-vis* other persons and beings. I can assume responsibility for my life and conduct. I can evaluate myself and my own moral stature. However, I can do none of this apart from others.

Relations with other people

We like to think of ourselves individualistically, but the fact is, we are integrally and necessarily related to others. We cannot exist without society. People are social beings. All that we do and have involves relationships with others, even when those others aren't close by. We are constantly responding to them in one way or another. We become persons only through relationships. And although we are individuals, all those relationships become part of us. Personal satisfaction, meaning, and well-being are highly dependent on the kinds and qualities of these relationships.

---

3. Kaufman, *In the Beginning*, 53–70.

Relations with other living things

Finally, although we often forget it, both as individuals and as society, we are totally dependent on nature, and, as we relate to other human beings we also relate to nonhuman forms of life. Not only this; we are *part* of nature. Yes, we are historical beings, but we also are biological beings. Kaufman calls us biohistorical beings.[4] Not only do we have a cultural relationship with nature and other creatures, we share a fundamental biological heritage.

These four dimensions represent what Franz Hinkelammert, a German philosopher and economist who has lived many years in Costa Rica, calls the "natural circuit of all life" because without this "circuit" of relationships, life is impossible.[5] Metaphorically these relationships are "metabolic" because they provide the energies and subsequent processing that make life—whether biological or cultural—possible. Theologically we can think of these dimensions as the *oikos* or "household" of God. *Oikos* is Greek for "habitat" or "house." These four relational dimensions are the basis of convivial life and together are the "place" where we live out our spirituality.

Of course these relationships are lived-out in real-life situations. In real life, these dimensions are always structured by power. Power too often is understood as "power over" others in order to achieve one's own interests, whether this is on the personal level or the level of political and social order. These power relationships determine opportunities and whole futures for individuals and peoples, even nonhuman creatures.

So spirituality—as does ethics—has a lot to do with power relations. A truly convivial life, life in the Spirit, would be deeply concerned for just relations in all dimensions of life. Only through just relationships can these dimensions truly be the natural circuit of life, convivial life.

Practice 2

For personal reflection

1. Sketch a diagram of all your relationships. Put yourself in the center. Around yourself write down every relationship you can think

---

4. Ibid., 42–44.
5. Hinkelammert, *El mapa del emperador*, 271.

Ethics and Spirituality

of. Don't forget that every time you speak to or pass by another person, whether it is a family member, friend, a store clerk, a coworker, you are relating to him or her. Many of these relationships are indirect and unknown personally. For example, some of your clothing was probably made in China or Central America, but through your clothing you are related to those seamstresses and tailors. Draw a line connecting each relationship with yourself. After drawing the diagram, analyze the following:

- Would it be possible to live without any of these relationships?
- What does each relationship signify for community life?
- What does each relationship signify for your personal life?
- Is there something missing in the diagram?
- What is different about the various relationships?
- How would you describe the quality of these relationships?

For group reflection

1. Compare your diagram with others in the group. How are they alike or different?
2. Discuss each of the four dimensions of "*convivencia*" or life-in-community. Why are they called the "natural circuit of all life" or "metabolic"? What are consequences of rupturing the "circuit"?
3. What could it mean to be guided by the Spirit among the relationships that are represented in the diagrams? What style of life or spirituality would be appropriate?

Step 2
Ethics and Spirituality for Life

Practice 3

For personal reflection

1. Ask five different people about the meaning of ethics. What do they understand by the term?

2. What is the purpose of ethics?

For group reflection

1. Share the answers you received when you asked people about ethics.
2. How do you relate spirituality and ethics?
3. It is possible to be spiritual but also unethical? Explain.

Your spirituality is about living in the *oikos* or household of God. You express it as you participate in *convivencia* or the natural circuit of all life. It should be evident, then, that spirituality urges a certain type of behavior. Behavior, of course, is what concerns ethics. So ethics and spirituality go together. We might even call ethics "spirituality for life."

Although ethics has to do with conduct, it doesn't signify primarily a list of "dos" and "don'ts." Rather, *ethics seeks to guide you in such a way that your behavior contributes responsibly to the upbuilding of community, and to the full development of the potentialities of people—including your own—and other forms of life.* In the context of community, ethics means to discern what is good and bad, right and wrong, responsible and appropriate for living in a loving fashion the many relationships that make up community. The forms or ways that ethics is so lived can differ from place to place and time to time, but its purpose of community-building remains.

Therefore ethics refers to the proposed conducts and actions, policies and social arrangements that we must put forward when we are living in real life situations. These should always favor and nourish our community lives, our personal lives, and the lives of others. Ethics not only has to do with the big decisions of life, but also everyday ones.

So the purpose of ethics is not so much to control behavior, but rather to guide you toward living purposefully, constructively, and joyfully. It has a lot to do with what philosopher-theologian John Caputo calls "passion of life" because ethics "lifts us up above the humdrum drift of indifference and mediocrity and gives us something surpassing to love beyond ourselves, something surpassing to seek beyond the empty consumerism of wandering through shopping malls in an endless search for more possessions."[6] Tillich calls this "seriousness." He tells us well that without

---

6. Caputo, *Philosophy and Theology*, 69.

Ethics and Spirituality

the "moral imperative," "[s]cience and the arts, politics, education—all become empty and self-destructive."[7] Such seriousness is the passion for life. So ethics really is about living life passionately and seriously. From the perspective of faith, ethics is the work of the Holy Spirit: guiding us to serious, passionate, loving, and fulfilling lives. This is spirituality for life.

Practice 4

For personal reflection

1. Review the answers you received in Practice 3 and list their common elements. What other elements are parts of ethics?
2. Draw a "house." That's where we live. Jesus reminded his listeners that a wise person will build a house upon a rock (read Matt 7:24–27). Build your house with the elements of ethics you found in Practice 3 (and the ones in the list below if you wish). Which ones go into the foundation? What will serve best for walls? Which elements make for strong roof?

   - Rules
   - Laws
   - Ideals
   - Values
   - Principles
   - Feelings
   - Decisions
   - Reasons
   - Science
   - Bible
   - Context
   - Relations[8]

---

7. Tillich, *Morality and Beyond*, 18.
8. This exercise is adapted from Pitt, *Choose*, 17–18.

Living According to the Spirit

3. Think about the ideas about ethics that your friends gave you (Practice 3) and compare them with the way I talk about ethics in the preceding paragraphs. How are they alike or different?
4. How do you understand Tillich's words that "Science and the arts, politics, education—all become empty and self-destructive if, in their creation, the moral imperative is disregarded"? What are some examples?
5. When were you in a situation in which you or someone you know endeavored to live ethics as the spirituality for life?

For group reflection

1. Share your house and other aspects of your personal reflection.
2. What would be the difference between ethics as guiding people toward constructive and meaningful lives and ethics as controlling people's behavior? Explain your answer.

Conversation 2

Ethical Problems and Spiritual Life

Practice 5

For personal reflection

1. List some of the ethical problems that you know in your community and country.
2. Why are they ethical problems? Who are the people or situations that are affected by them? How are they affected?

For group reflection

1. Share the ethical problems you have identified.
2. What makes a problem "ethical"? What does it have to do with spirituality?

When we look around (at ourselves, our families, communities, businesses, governments, and many other dimensions of life) the shirking of responsibility is all too evident! People just don't seem to care about anyone but themselves. As a world community, nations are still divided, especially between rich and poor. Even in our own country such divisions exist. Most people who suffer unemployment are African or Hispanic Americans. This reality shows how racism, intended or not, continues to divide us. Women still receive lower wages for the same work a man does. Immigrants, especially those without proper immigration papers, are lambasted as threats to national security. The natural environment, with

Ethical Problems and Spiritual Life

its animals and plants, too often is subordinated to pressing "economic" or "security" needs. Then there are the so-called personal problems of drug addiction, pornography, and spouses cheating on each other. Many people evade paying taxes and look for any other ways of getting around the law for personal gain. This list could go on and on. These are ethical problems. They all affect communities. They prevent convivial living. As Saint Paul would say, they are "works of the flesh" (Gal 5:19).

In summary, ethical problems are questions that affect life-in-community, *convivencia* or *koinonia*. They are the things that rupture the natural circuit that gives life to persons and communities. They prevent convivial living. In one form or another, they have to do with our relationships. Don't forget that ethics always has to do with our relationship to God, ourselves, other people, and other living beings. Thus what is ethical or what is antiethical is defined in terms of our relationships and their capacity to be life-giving.

Step 1
Who Is My Neighbor?

A very common ethical problem is the way people are excluded. We see this exclusion when people are not respected and used only for personal benefits and pleasures, or because they make us afraid. It is manifested when we think that others are not as important as ourselves, or not "like me" and so don't deserve the same rights and respect. I'm sure you can think of many ways exclusion occurs, especially of people who are "different." It's easy to love and respect persons who are like us and with whom we agree. But what if they are different? What if they are a different color? What if they speak a different language? What if they have a different sexual orientation? What if they follow a different religion? This leads to the question the Pharisee asked Jesus, "Who is my neighbor"?

Read Luke 10:29–37 and Romans 13:8–10.

The Pharisee's question is the fundamental question of Christian ethics: who is my neighbor, or more correctly, to whom am I a neighbor? Peruvian theologian Gustavo Gutiérrez explains:

Ethics and Spirituality

> The parable of the Good Samaritan ends with the famous inversion which Christ makes of the original question. They asked him, "Who is my neighbor?" and when everything seemed to point to the wounded man in the ditch on the side of road, Christ asked, "Which of these three do you think was neighbor to the man who fell into the hands of the robbers?" (Luke 10:29, 36). The neighbor was the Samaritan who *approached* the wounded man and *made him his neighbor.* The neighbor, as has been said, is not the one whom I find in my path, but rather the one in whose path I place myself, the one to whom I approach and actively seek.[1]

For ethics, the question about the neighbor is fundamental. Jesus taught, "You shall love your neighbor as yourself" (Matt 22:39) and Saint Paul explained that all the requirements of Christian ethics "are summed up" by these same words (Rom 13:9).

Neighbors respect each other. They don't rob, cheat, lie, or exploit one another. They don't harm each other. Neighbors do everything possible to help out. They include each other in their communities. At the same time they respect each other's integrity and autonomy. Saint Paul affirms, "Love does no wrong to a neighbor" (Rom 13:10). Who, then, is your neighbor? You have to decide, but don't forget: your neighbor is never just someone who lives close by. Your neighbor can be anybody, and that's the rub!

Our tendency is to avoid someone who's not like us, or, if they live far away just not worry about them at all. Too often we think that a person who we perceive as "different"—because she or he isn't part of our group, has a different lifestyle, is a different sex or has a different sexual orientation, political party, religion, nationality, or social class, or race—somehow doesn't merit the same ethical obligations we have toward our "own." Frequently not even our families are treated as neighbors, as evidenced by domestic violence. And increasingly we see this exclusion oriented toward immigrants, especially those without proper documents!

But Jesus's and Saint Paul's teachings about neighborliness demonstrate that Christian spirituality leads us toward others, even—especially—those who are "different." Gutiérrez reminds us that Christian spirituality "will center on a *conversion* to the neighbor, the oppressed person, the exploited social class, the despised ethnic group, the dominated country."

---

1. Gutiérrez, *Theology of Liberation*, 198.

Ethical Problems and Spiritual Life

He calls this "a spirituality for liberation."[2] (Remember Isa 58?) Such spirituality leads us to find the face of God in the face of the other person.

Exclusion—the rejection of neighborliness—is very hurtful and destructive. Exclusion ruptures convivial life or *koinonia*.

Practice 6

For personal reflection

1. Put the parable of the Good Samaritan in today's world, in your own city or town. What persons or groups could be identified with the persons in the parable? Who is the wounded man, the Samaritan, the robbers, etc.? Indicate your answers in the following diagram:

    - The wounded person
    - The Samaritan
    - The robbers
    - The priest or Levite
    - The owner of the hotel
    - The Samaritan's animal[3]

For group reflection

1. Share your diagram with the others.
2. What does being a neighbor mean in today's world? What does it mean to be a Good Samaritan in today's world?
3. Who and why are there "different" people in your community?
4. Why is it difficult to get close to those who are perceived as different?
5. What attitudes are proper for ethics as spirituality for life?

---

2. Ibid., 204–5.
3. This exercise is adapted from Pitt, *Choose*, 35.

Ethics and Spirituality

Step 2
Spirituality and Community

Spiritual life takes form in relation to other people and living beings. It is through these relationships that we discover our true potentialities as persons created in the image and likeness of God. Likewise, through their relation to us other persons are able to find and to live their own potential as children of God. This is because, as Tillich explains, we become truly persons only "within a community of persons." Each person's responsibility is great because we influence the lives of others.

This is very evident in our person-to-person relationships. Parents influence their children. Our friends influence our personal and social behavior.

But spiritual life isn't limited to our person-to-person relations. It has everything to do with our collective or social relations. Spiritual life also is about community life. It leads to concern about social and environmental justice. It seeks loving, caring relationships among different races and ethnic groups, and those who are "different." Spiritual life struggles against social hate in order to create societies that practice tolerance and acceptance.

Community relations imply political and economic policies. Politics and economics organize our communities. This means that ethics, as spirituality for life, has to do with politics and the economy. The way in which a society is organized significantly determines the possibilities that people and groups have to develop their own potential as children of God. Through society spirituality takes concrete form.

Spirituality is fundamentally about building convivial community.

Practice 7

For personal reflection

1. Read Luke 4:16–21. In the Gospel account, this is Jesus's first sermon. It is his "manifesto" as the Son of God. Jesus refers to different groups of persons or social categories. We can find these persons and groups today.

Ethical Problems and Spiritual Life

Thinking about your city or country, who are the following?
- The poor
- The brokenhearted
- The captives
- The blind
- The oppressed[4]

2. What does this passage say about society? What kind of ethics would be needed to change this reality into a true *koinonia*? What does it imply for spirituality?

3. Use the following table to analyze the quality of your personal relations. To the left is a list of personal relations. Above are indicated some characteristics of relationships. Add other personal relations or characteristics, if you like. If a relationship is positive, mark 1 in the corresponding space, mark 2 if is more or less good, and 3 if it is bad.

Relationship	Love	Confidence	Equality	Faithful
Father				
Mother				
Daughter/Son				
Spouse				
Relatives				
Colleagues				
Teacher/Professor				
Beggars				
Employees/Employers				
Yourself				

Are you satisfied with what the diagram reveals about your relationships? Do you need to make some changes? Why? What does the diagram teach about life-in-community?

---

4. This exercise is adapted from Pitt, *Choose*, 39.

Ethics and Spirituality

Step 3
Spiritual and Ethical Formation

A person isn't born with ethics and spirituality. These are learned in the course of our lives through our many relationships. It is a process that begins in the first weeks of life. Generally it is an unconscious and unanalyzed process. It just occurs. It is based on the silent teachings of our parents, relatives, friends, schools, churches, and communications media.

This process in which we develop ethical and spiritual values sociologists call "socialization." This is the slow but constant incorporation of a person into a particular society or community or group. A person internalizes the group's or society's values and ethics, along with their meanings as understood by the group.

This process is constant, from birth to old age. We are always learning and changing and adapting. And although much is unconscious, we are not passive recipients. Each person, in his or her own way, actively participates. We interpret and adapt "social learnings" in novel ways that make them our own.

But in order to shape your life, you have to become aware of it. You need to analyze and take stock of what's happening to you and what you are doing. Otherwise you just sort of float along and don't take life passionately and seriously.

Now there are lots of aspects that are very influential in forming us ethically and spiritually. But the key to good ethics and solid spirituality is the quality of our affective life. Being accepted and trusted—and accepting and trusting—is basic. It is here that your basic predisposition toward all relationships is formed. This is the beginning of moral conscience.

Practice 8

For personal reflection

1. What does "conscience" mean for you? Where does it come from? How do you know the difference between good and bad? Where does the capacity to discern right and wrong come from?
2. How is the conscience formed? What importance does daily life have in its formation? How would you go about creating a good conscience?

Moral conscience

The idea of "conscience" is very similar to the concept of "heart" in the Hebrew Bible. There we find that, together with wisdom, the "heart" is the center of feelings and represents the true person. It expresses the relationship between a person and God. (Read Ps 26 and Ps 49:1–4). The Gospels don't mention conscience; nevertheless Saint Paul and his followers often refer to it. (See for example: 1 Cor 4:4; 8:7; 10:25; 2 Cor 1:12; Rom 2:15; 9:1; 13:5; 1 Tim 1:5, 19; 3:9; Titus 1:15.)

The conscience isn't biological like an arm or leg. Rather, it is socially and culturally formed through social relations. This means that the conscience can be problematic. Predominant cultural values and social ideas may not be worthy to follow. Just because culture and society "teach" something doesn't automatically mean that it's good. Besides, cultures and societies teach many things, sometimes contradictory things. The conscience must be cultivated, taught to discern what is worthy and what is not. Only a conscience that can do this will produce good, moral fruit.

The conscience is valuable because it reminds us of the importance of ethical sensibility for living seriously, passionately, and convivially. It brings together our values, basic options, and commitments. It orients our behavior in relation to the natural circuit of all life. It calls us to take responsibility for ourselves and communities. It guides us toward others and actions that contribute to life-in-community.

Your conscience is the foundation of your ethical character. Character refers to "being." It becomes your basic orientation toward life and forms your behavior. It brings together your beliefs and actions into a coherent whole. Your character establishes the priorities, commitments, and interests that govern you as a person living among many others.

Historically, the church has defined character in terms of "virtues." This idea has its origin among the ancient Greeks and their concern for prudence, moderation, courage, and justice. These are known as the "cardinal virtues" because the Greeks thought they were foundational of all others. However the great thirteenth–century philosopher Thomas Aquinas incorporated these cardinal virtues under the "theological virtues" of faith, hope, and love (1 Cor 13:13). These cardinal and theological virtues are, to a large extent, the basis of spirituality and ethics. They are predispositions that guide actions, decisions, and relations.

Ethics and Spirituality

The wisdom of history teaches that the way to a virtuous life is to practice it—that is, live it. Through practice virtues are incorporated into character. Many great religious traditions, including Christianity, affirm "spiritual exercises" or "disciplines." These are techniques that, if practiced regularly, help a person become aware of virtues and other spiritual values. They thus become natural habits. They help people experience the sacred and to express it in daily life.

Well known are works by Thomas à Kempis (1380–1471) and Ignatius of Loyola (1491–1556). Kempis wrote a series of meditations on how to shape life as an "imitation of Christ" because "anyone who wishes to understand Christ's words and to savor them fully should strive to become like him in every way."[5] The "spiritual exercises" of Ignatius of Loyola are a series of introspections, meditations, and contemplations, usually to be experienced during a four-week retreat. Their purpose is, according to Ignatius, "to seek and to find the divine will in the ordering of one's life with a view to the salvation of one's soul."[6] Unfortunately these spiritual exercises often have been understood as ways to distance oneself from the world and history. But that's not what Ignatius meant. Father Ignacio Ellacuría, a Jesuit priest who ministered in El Salvador, "was a man passionately committed to Ignatian spirituality." He said that spiritual exercises should be "contemplation in action."[7] For him, only in the world and through history do the exercises make sense because it is there that God is encountered. For Father Ellacuría, the spiritual exercises of Ignatius lead you to act in the world. In 1989, because of Father Ellacuría's commitment to the poor and social justice, the El Salvadoran army murdered him.

John Wesley, the founder of Methodism, did not refer to spiritual exercises or disciplines. But he affirmed the importance of what he called, "means of grace." According to this great eighteenth-century evangelist, through constant participation in Holy Communion, Bible study, prayer, and fasting, in addition to visiting and serving the poor and needy, one would experience the power of grace and thus experience "the renewal of your soul in righteousness and true holiness."[8] Like Father Ellacuría,

---

5. Kempis, *Imitation of Christ*, 3.
6. Longridge, *Spiritual Exercises*, 4.
7. Ashley, "Contemplation in the Action," 144–45.
8. Wesley, "Means of Grace," 396–97.

spirituality, for Wesley, implies the integration of love and commitment to others as a whole style of life. This, without doubt, would be a virtuous life.

Spirituality "condenses" moral conscience, virtues, and character into a whole. It implies a way of "practicing" life, a manner of living in community with God, oneself, other persons, and other living things. Surely this is ethics: living in such a way that divine will is manifested.

CONVERSATION 3

Ethical and Spiritual Values

IN THIS SECTION I want to explore ethical and spiritual values because they undergird and orient ethical discernment and spiritual life. Your values determine to a large degree your ethical conclusions and proposals. Values are like pillars or cross beams holding up your church sanctuary or another big building. They keep you from being indifferent. They commit you to other persons and life projects. So, for persons and their communities values are those qualities that are considered of fundamental importance. They orient and justify conduct or behavior.

But it's very difficult to know exactly how values are defined or what they mean specifically. Nor is there general agreement about what a particular value might mean. Values even can be defined in different ways. This is one of the reasons values are so powerful! Furthermore, a value that served 500 years ago perhaps isn't adequate at all in today's times. So it's also necessary that values constantly be redefined and reshaped so that they are adequate to new situations.

Indeed, new values have to be created. For example, years ago, when the world's population was small and technology rudimentary, caring for the natural environment wasn't an important value. It wasn't necessary because there wasn't any danger. Today the situation is dramatically different. The population is huge and consumes enormous amounts of energy and other resources. Modern technology often has proven to be extremely damaging. Animal habitats are destroyed or damaged and with that, the animals themselves. Our communities are adversely affected. So we're learning to value the natural order. "Green" has become a universal value!

In the past women were valued mainly as mothers, housewives, and caregivers. High value was placed on being a mother. Women were

Ethical and Spiritual Values

identified with and valued for their feminine biology. Subsidiary values such as submissiveness to men, were created to reinforce these principal ones. A woman's "place" was the home in order to take care of her husband and children. But today the context is very different. The population is big and doesn't require large families. Indeed, fewer children are needed! At the same time, the modern economic world requires women to be in the paid workforce. Above all, women are increasingly accepted as equal to men. Women can be "producers" as well as "reproducers." So new values pertaining to women have emerged. These values are not so much in reference to biology, as to intellectual, creative, and critical capacities. These new values change old values, such as female submissiveness to men.

Finally, in previous times, only the elite had opportunities to visit other cultures or meet peoples of different religions and nationalities. Cultural, religious, and linguistic homogeneity was highly valued. Whatever was different was excluded. But with globalization all this changes. Cultural interchange—massive immigration, travel, instantaneous news reporting, Internet, student exchanges, mission work teams—puts us face-to-face with peoples who often are very different. The old value of cultural homogeneity is now detrimental because it can't respond to this new reality. So new values such as diversity, multiculturalism, interreligious dialogue, and tolerance and acceptance of those who are different, have become very important. Without them, we can't have convivial communities.

There are, of course, lots of others. These are just examples. Take a minute and think about how values are changing.

Because of these changes there is a lot of talk about the crisis of values or loss of values. Values change, for good or bad, because life changes. Technology offers new possibilities (birth control and stem cell therapy). The economy takes different directions (free trade and off shore contracting). New ideas about the future of humanity emerge (international borders are increasingly fluid). Novel ways of living, learning, and being come about (home schooling and different models of family life). As a result, many people lose moral direction. Others seek new ways of living. All this produces crisis.

It's important to remember that crisis signifies opportunity. Changes in values are not always bad. Although the change may be painful, it just might be very good. Think about the old and valued "whites only" world of racial segregation! The crisis in values is the opportunity to re-define what living together means. It permits taking seriously new problems and new possibilities. The crisis helps us constructively face the future.

So values emerge—are created—through historical processes, interaction with nature and each other. They come from culture, socio-political and economic organization. Ideologies propose values, as do religions. As Christians, major sources of our values are God as the very Ground of Being, the scriptures as testimony to faith, and the faith communities and traditions where the Christian life has been formed and lived, as well as the capacity to reason that God has so generously given us. I'm not saying that we have to retake past values. Rather, we return to these sources and others in order to construct new ethical and spiritual values valid and useful for today's realities.

Step 1
Sin, World, and Flesh

Practice 9

For personal reflection

1. Talk to various people in your church about the religious and ethical meaning of the words "sin," "world," and "flesh."
2. How do they define the significance of these terms? What do their definitions have to do with spirituality?

For group reflection

3. Compare the answers you received with members of the group.

In the New Testament traditions unethical conduct often is expressed as "sin," "world," and "flesh." Let's think about what these traditional terms mean and how they are related to ethics and spirituality.

Sin

Sin means a life separated from God, one's self, and others. Such separation is evil because it doesn't allow responsible living-in-community.

Ethical and Spiritual Values

It signifies centering on one's self instead of turning toward others. This "deep" meaning of sin is manifested in our conduct, in what we often call "sins." The New Testament calls this "missing the mark," as an archer misses the target. Our conduct is "off target" because our lives are "off target." Jesus rarely used the word, but for Saint Paul it is a favorite. In the Hebrew Scriptures, sin refers above all to the community's relationship with Yahweh and faithfulness to the Covenant Code. When we integrate the New Testament concepts of sin with that of the Hebrew Scripture, we see very clearly that sin is always personal and communal.

Nearly always sin is expressed relationally. That is, the Bible uses it in terms of convivial life with God and others. Sin refers to conduct that goes against the kinds of relationships that are required for positive and responsible life together. So sin signals actions and attitudes that lead to rupture, alienation, and disrespect for the dignity, integrity, and wellbeing of others. It includes conscious and consented irresponsibility, as well as the exclusion and domination of others in order to maintain or to assure group and personal privileges. Thus the deep meaning of sin signifies everything that separates us from God, ourselves, and others who are also part of God's creation.

Thus sin is never just personal or individual. Missing the mark has social implications. Mudge says, "Every private moral issue also has a public meaning. The line between public and private becomes increasingly hard to draw."[1] This is because sin damages not only ourselves but also other people and convivial life including the natural order. So "personal sin" has a social dimension: it hurts others. We sin *against* others. At the same time, sin institutionalizes itself as social, political, and economic relations. In this sense, sin "escapes" the individual and penetrates the way community life is organized. This "structural sin" manifests itself as exploitation (cheap labor) and discrimination (limiting life opportunities because of one's sex, race, national origin, or language). It is manifested in policies that benefit some people but hurt others. It is always expressed in gender, racial, ethnic, and economic inequality. All this is social sin.

When the biblical writers use the words "world" and "flesh" with a negative connotation, they are referring to social or structural sin. In biblical times, the modern sociological concept of "society" didn't exist, so the idea of "social sin" didn't either. But society did exist and the biblical

---

1. Mudge, *Church as Moral Community*, 89.

writers were acutely aware of the social dimension of sin. They chose "world" and "flesh" to express this concern. They symbolize social and ethical concepts expressed theologically. But there is something deeper. The biblical writers saw that sin penetrated their own societies in a very totalitarian manner.

World and flesh

What does "world" mean when it's used in the Bible? In first place, it refers to where God's salvific activity takes place: the concrete, earthly living space where people are people. Salvation is not other worldly; it is this worldly. God in Jesus Christ "gives life to the world" (John 6:33) and saves it (John 3:17). Thus spiritual life doesn't take you out of the world. It takes you deeply into the world through your struggling to recreate the world itself. "For God so loved the world" (John 3:16), showing us that the deepest value is love. Spirituality in the world leads to communities founded on mutual love.

But it is also clear that "world" has a negative sense for the biblical writers. They tell us that we shouldn't live according to the world (John 8:36; 1 Cor 2:12, 11:32; 1 John 4:4–6). Followers of Christ aren't part of the world. What did they mean when they wrote this? What could they mean today?

In Greek—the original language of the New Testament—the world (*kosmos*) isn't mainly a geographical place. Rather, it means "order" or "organization." It has to do with the way something is formed, organized, or arranged. The word "cosmetic" comes from *kosmos* or world. Its biblical use refers to social order arranged or constituted by human beings. Its negative sense points to the evil ways societies are put together. In this sense, world refers to injustice and assumes a socio-political character beyond individual actions. It represents all that is contrary to love and justice. That's why Jesus tells Pilate, "My kingdom is not from this world" (John 18:36).

The Bible doesn't consider the world to be bad as such. Rather, that the world is dominated by evil. It is society organized in sinful ways. Material order isn't impure (Rom 14:14; 1 Cor 10:23–26). Rather the New Testament uses "world" to indicate human society separated from God and dominated by egoism and hatred.

Ethical and Spiritual Values

The same can be said about the biblical use of "flesh." The Greek word (*sarx*) clearly refers to the biological body, but Saint Paul's use of the word refers to ethics. "Flesh" isn't evil in itself. It's the conduct of the flesh that concerns Saint Paul. Spirituality doesn't mean escaping bodily, material reality by denying the needs and pleasures of the body or seeing it as bad. It means orienting the body toward those values we find in Jesus Christ as the prototype of the new humanity.

Today, when we speak of society or sin, we don't use terms like "world" and "flesh." Instead, we talk about social injustice, social class, sexism, racism, economic policies, taxation, international relations, and so on. With the emergence of the sciences, especially the social sciences, we understand society and evil in different ways. Nevertheless, the biblical language reminds us that sin is not limited to individuals. It penetrates the totality of life.

Practice 10

For personal reflection

1. Find ten biblical passages that are about physical wellbeing, that is, the body and its needs. Some of the texts should be from the Gospels and the life of Jesus. Analyze each one. Why is physical wellbeing important in the text? How does Jesus respond to the needs of the body? What can we learn for our own response to "the flesh"?

Ethics and Spirituality

2. What does your church say about sin? How is it defined? Use the following table to make notes about some biblical texts about sin.[2]

	What's happening?	How is sin understood?	How does Jesus respond?	How should we respond?
Gen 4:1–16				
Gen 11:1–9				
Exod 32				
Deut 30:15–20				
Jer 5:20–29				
Matt 25:31–46				
Mark 2:1–12				
Luke 15:1–31				
John 8:1–11				
Rom 6:15–23				

3. How would you summarize "sin" according to these texts?

For group reflection

1. Share your personal answers with the group.
2. Read out loud the following texts, substituting the word "world" with "sinful social order" or "structures of domination": 1 John 4:5, 19; John 18:36; 1 Corinthians 2:12; 1 Corinthians 11:32. Share your reactions.
3. What can we learn about living in the world? What does this have to do with ethics?

2. This exercise is adapted from Koll, *Teología evangélica*, 46.

Step 2
Bible, Church, and Values

For Christianity, two principal sources of values and ethics are the Bible and the Church. These sources represent the foundation and historical context of our faith. Other important sources, historically, are reason and experience.

Bible

Clearly the Bible is a source, if not the source, of Christian ethics, but it's not a book of ethical recipes. It's not a manual of behavior that we can just apply mechanically to life's problems. The authors of the Bible lived in times very different from ours. We live 2,000 years after Jesus, in totally distinct cultures and historical contexts. Lots of problems we face now didn't even exist in biblical days. For example: contraceptives; smoking tobacco; genetic manipulation; free trade economic policies; computers, computer games, and internet; and medical technology that can prolong life mechanically. The ethical orientation or directives found in the Bible were directed to the concrete situations of those times. Altogether, the oldest to the youngest scripture represents a period of about 1,500 years. These scriptures weren't even recognized as such until about 1,700 years ago when the Church formally recognized the Bible we have today. This means that the scriptures contain many ideas and beliefs that no longer exist because of new experience and knowledge.

At the same time, partially because of its development in very different times, not all the material contained in the Bible is of equal importance. Some parts are not normative, for example, Deuteronomy 21:18–21 or Matthew 18:6. We don't kill our children when they disobey, even though the Bible commands us to do so! Another example is the imperative written by a follower of Saint Paul, "Let a woman learn in silence with full submission" (1 Tim 2:11). The commands to commit violence, the accepted patriarchy and social hierarchy, and evident ethnocentrism that many biblical texts presume, must be questioned and rejected as having divine authority.

Indeed, the Bible doesn't contain just a single ethical stance. This is clear when we contrast Jesus's command to "love one another" with the command to kill rebellious children. Saint Paul's affirmation that "There is no longer Jew or Greek, there is no longer slave or free, there is no longer male and female; for all of you belong in Christ Jesus" (Gal 3:28) contradicts the words about women found in 1 Timothy and other biblical texts. Furthermore, the Bible is composed of a great variety of material presented in diverse literary forms. There are sermons, poems, letters, metaphors and symbols, parables, and commands. There are stories, myths, and histories. Sometimes the Bible is very specific and other times very general. The authors are distinct, each with their own concerns.

It's important to recognize this diversity in order to read the Bible adequately. This will help you discern which material contains authority and how it does so. The diversity itself is enriching and will stimulate your moral imagination. Only as you *study* the Bible will you find it useful.

The Bible is the historic memory of the faith that shows how God's revelation was understood and interpreted in a particular time and place. It is the testimony and confession of faith. In this historic memory, we seek the character and basic structures of the moral life. We always ask, what is the basic concern of the author?

You read the biblical texts from the perspective of your own times. You want to find biblical guidance for today. To do so you have to dialogue with the ancient texts. Constant dialogue will provoke your moral imagination and you will be oriented as you walk through life today. Here you will discover theological categories and frameworks. These will organize and illuminate your ethical conduct. More than specific mandates, the Bible teaches the founding values and orienting principles that are to guide you. These help you clarify God's will in your own situation. In this sense, the Bible is the necessary and authoritative source of Christian ethics today.

Practice 11

For personal reflection

1. In what ways do you think the Bible is authoritative? When different people read the Bible, do all understand the text in the same way? What factors influence how someone interprets the Bible and its ethical orientations?

Ethical and Spiritual Values

2. For you personally, how do you find the Bible helpful when you face difficult life situations?
3. The following is a list of some moral rules that are found in the Bible. After reading the texts, which of the rules do you consider valid for today and which ones seem to be directed only to the time they were written? Why do you accept some biblical rules but not all of them?

    - Exodus 20:1–17 (Deut 5:1–21)
    - Exodus 21:12–25
    - Exodus 22:16–31
    - Leviticus 15:1–33
    - Leviticus 20:1–27
    - Deuteronomy 15:1–23
    - Deuteronomy 22:13–30
    - Deuteronomy 24:14–25
    - Deuteronomy 25:5–10
    - Matthew 5:27–48 (Luke 6:27–36)
    - Matthew 7:12
    - Matthew 22:34–40 (Mark 12:28–34)
    - Matthew 25:31–46
    - Mark 9:42–49
    - Mark 10:1–12 (Matt 19:1–12; Luke 16:18)
    - John 13:31–35
    - Romans 12:1–21
    - Romans 13:1–14
    - 1 Corinthians 7:1–40
    - 1 Corinthians 11:2–16
    - Galatians 3:26–28
    - Galatians 5:1–6, 13–15
    - 1 Thessalonians 5:12–14

Ethics and Spirituality

For group reflection

1. Share your conclusions after your study of biblical rules. Explain your reasons. What does this study of these rules teach about the Bible and ethics?
2. What values are manifested in these moral rules?

Church

Above all the Church defines the founding values of the Christian life. Of course each Christian interprets and appropriates the Bible and the experience of God personally. But the Church represents the Christian communion. It is the "body of Christ" that unites Christians today with Christians of other times and places. The Church, through its many denominations, develops formal teachings or doctrines about values and ethics. Its own internal life also proposes values to be followed. In this sense, the Church represents the historic wisdom and communion of the followers of Jesus Christ. This is the meaning of tradition. Thus tradition becomes the basis for following Christ even today.

The Church, however, is a communion of diverse gifts, histories, and beliefs. This means that there will always be a diversity of ways to understand values and ethics within the Church itself. Denominations will differ. There will be differences within each denomination. So just as in the Bible, there is no single definition of Christian values and ethics. But in the Church, as the Christian communion, followers of Christ meet in mutual confidence for dialogue together about the content and requirements of the Christian life or Christian ethics. We share our differences in order to grow together in faith. This is another way the Church is the source of values.

Experience and reason

Other historic sources of values for Christian spirituality are experience and reason. Experience is both individual and collective. That is, we live our own lives, but we do so as part of groups. We are part of cultures, and we share gender and racial characteristics, among others. These collective experiences are produced and shaped historically. If viewed critically, experience shows us how to best respond to different situations. Experience puts things into proper perspective. It provides clues for timing—knowing when to do something. Knowing what has happened before helps us to understand what to do when we are again in a similar situation. It helps us discern what is good and useful. Experience confirms whether something is true. Indeed, values don't exist apart from experience. They're real when they're practiced. So understanding critically experience, individual as well as collective, is a vital source of orientation. Reason is the faculty for gaining and understanding knowledge. It processes information for living. Through reason we can think critically, analyze situations, and discern strengths and weaknesses among different options and actions. Through reason we can create and enrich values.

Practice 12

For personal reflection

1. How does the Church teach values and ethics?
2. Why is the communion of believers important for ethical orientation?
3. How should reason influence ethics?
4. Have your own experiences influenced your way of ethical thinking? Explain.

For group reflection

1. What are some differences that you know of among the churches on ethics?
2. Why do these differences exist?
3. Is it good or bad that churches don't always agree? Why?

Step 3
Values for a Spirituality for Life

What are the ethical values that provide direction to a spirituality for life? There are many biblical texts that give clues for answering this question.

Ethics and Spirituality

I'm going to concentrate on Galatians. This letter written by Saint Paul gives some especially rich clues to follow. Before going on, please read Galatians 5:13–26.

According to Saint Paul, freedom and love are the foundation of ethics (Gal 5:13). Coercion (the "law") isn't the basis for real responsibility. It doesn't allow action to surge from deep inside or the heart. Under coercion, a person acts out of obligation, not commitment. But when freedom or liberty is the basis for ethics, actions come from internal commitment. We act not out of obligation but from conviction. For Saint Paul, freedom signifies commitment to love: "do not use your freedom as an opportunity for self-indulgence, but through love become slaves to one another" (Gal 5:13).

The Apostle goes on to distinguish "works" and "fruits": the former destroy community and the latter build up community. We have seen that *koinonia* (convivial life or community) is a fundamental concern for Saint Paul. He defines the values and conduct appropriate to Christian living in the context of *koinonia*.

Galatians 5:19–21—"the works of the flesh"—is a list of behaviors that clearly are detrimental to convivial life. Saint Paul understands them as the result of slavery to one's own desires. They are behaviors that break confidence and loyalty. They signify exploitation and selfishness. They exclude others because they don't respect other people's integrity, dignity, and autonomy. Such behaviors imply that others are only things or objects that can be manipulated for one's own benefit. At bottom, they are behaviors that abuse others. In no way do they express love. No community can survive if such behavior is its basis.

By contrast, Galatians 5:22–24 describes "the fruit" that facilitate *koinonia* or convivial life. Such fruit is free, because it comes from unselfish motives: it comes from the heart. It generates trust and confidence, loyalty, and community. It facilitates dialogue. It is oriented toward the wellbeing of others. Such fruit is behavior that is respectful of others. This is truly ethics for living-in-community. Persons committed to Jesus Christ will live by that kind of morality because they are free.

Saint Paul teaches us that the basic values of Christian ethics—those that are to give direction to spirituality—are those that foment convivial life: freedom, love, joy, kindness, faithfulness, humility, self-control. We can add others: honesty and transparency, responsibility, justice, wellbeing, tolerance, equality, and equity. And there are more. These are the

Ethical and Spiritual Values

values that construct community. Spirituality means living these values. Christian ethics is about positive, respectful, and loving relationships in all dimensions of life.

Practice 13

For personal reflection

1. List the values you believe are basic for convivial living. Answer the following questions about your list:
    - Why are they values?
    - Does everyone understand these values in the same way? Why?
    - Are some values specifically Christian, or can non-Christians also live by them?
    - How do they help convivial living?
    - Where do these values come from?

For group reflection

1. Share and discuss your answers together.
2. Modeling values can help you understand them more clearly. Here's an exercise: In the center of a sheet of paper, write the name of a value you consider important. Then around the value, (1) write similar values (maybe even synonyms), (2) what it is important about the value, (3) what benefits it offers, (4) some examples of how the value is practiced, (5) what its limitations are, and (6) even some opposite or conflicting values. This is a good group exercise. Do it for several different values.[3]

---

3. This exercise is adapted from Hall, *Moral Education*, 63, 72–73.

Conversation 4

Biblical and Spiritual Ethics

As I have said, there are many biblical resources that inform ethics as spirituality for life. So far I've relied mostly on Saint Paul, especially his letter to the Galatians. Now I want to include a couple of other key texts: Micah 6:6–8 and Luke 10:29–37.

I've selected these two biblical texts because they are paradigm or model texts. This means that they synthesize and summarize the central teachings that are found in a great diversity of texts. They are models or paradigms because they exhibit what is basic to the great traditions of faith. Also, they are simple and direct. They stimulate our moral imagination. They provoke us to live a certain lifestyle. They propose the foundations of ethics as spirituality for convivial life.

Step 1
Social Justice and the Prophetic Tradition

The Prophets are deep tradition in the Hebrew Bible. They influence much of ancient Israelite teaching. These prophetic voices are fundamentally concerned for justice. Jesus identified himself with the prophets, and so much of Christian teaching also is about justice.

Practice 14

For personal reflection

1. What does justice mean for you? Give some examples of justice and injustice that you have seen in your own community.

Biblical and Spiritual Ethics

2. How can we know if something is just? That is, what makes something to be just or unjust?
3. Based on what you know about the Hebrew Prophets, what do they teach about justice?

For group reflection

1. What is meant by "social" justice?
2. What does justice have to do with ethics? What does it have to do with spirituality?
3. What are some practical implications of justice as an ethical value? What does justice imply for faithful living?

Read Micah 6:6–8. This text summarizes the whole prophetic tradition. It's based on the ideas, teaching, and theology of Exodus and Deuteronomy. It emphasizes liberation and social justice. The widow, orphan, and immigrant are especially protected by Yahweh. According to these teachings, justice always is bent in favor of the socially and economically unprotected.

The prophet Micah lived some 750 years before Jesus Christ, during the same time as Isaiah, Amos, and Hosea. Micah was a peasant from Judah where Jerusalem is located. He announced God's judgment on Jerusalem because it had ceased to practice justice. It exploited the poor. The rights of widows, orphans, and immigrants weren't respected. Micah also condemned violence and war. Although the prophet's message is hard, it also recalls the mercy of God. God forgives and restores. A future of justice and peace is promised. According to Micah, these are the foundations for ethics.

Verses 6 to 8 make clear that life faithful to God isn't based on attending worship services. Nor does it consist of certain specifically religious activities. Rather, the faithful life is a whole way of living with others. For this reason Micah proposes three foundations or values for ethics as spirituality for convivial life: justice, love and kindness, and humility. A life acceptable to God is built around these foundations.

Ethics and Spirituality

Justice

Justice—in the Bible often translated to English as righteousness—is basic to the Hebrew Bible. It is a theme that passes through all the writings but is present especially in the Prophets. It is rooted in the liberation of the Hebrews from Egyptian slavery. Because God liberates the people of Israel, God is proclaimed the God of justice.

In the Hebrew Bible, "justice" refers equally to divine or human action. Above all, it signifies defending the poor and their rights to basic necessities and fair treatment. It is to advocate for their wellbeing (Deut 10:18–19), because God vindicates the oppressed and defends the weak. Justice always has the sense of right and judgment, of help and freedom. Its purpose is to create and preserve convivial community. These ideas of justice are reflected in the various versions of Micah 6:8. For example, the New Revised Standard Version (NRSV) says "to do justice," "to love kindness," and "to walk humbly." The Good News Bible (GNT) reads, "to do what is just, to show constant love, and to live in humble fellowship with our God." The Living Bible (LB) proposes, "to be fair and just and merciful, and to walk humbly with your God." All emphasize *doing* justice.

The justice that Micah has in mind is not neutral. It is actively taking the side of the poor, the dispossessed, and the weak. Micah's justice is dynamic. It is creative because it requires changed relationships. "To do justice" means correcting economic, political, and social inequalities. Take time to read some of the prophets. Listen to Isaiah, Amos, Jeremiah, and Hosea. They say the same thing. Even today the unfair practices and unjust relationships the prophets mention are a reality. Economic policies favor the rich. In spite of great changes, social discrimination still exists based on race and gender and ethnic group and social class. Xenophobia (fear of those who are different) colors relationships with people of different nationalities and languages. Women and children suffer violence and other abuse. Homosexual people are degraded and denied basic rights. The natural environment and other living creatures are abused and hurt. I bet you've witnessed some of these in your own community! Biblical justice calls us to correct such injustices.

Micah is very clear: justice is the fundamental value that is viewed by God as "good."

Mercy and kindness

The Hebrew word for mercy and kindness is rich with meaning and hard to translate with a single English word. The Hebrew is *hesed* and signifies a relationship of commitment. It implies fidelity, loyalty, obligation, and mutual help. It also means to be rescued or to be saved, depending on the context. It often is translated as love. The New Revised Standard Version (NRSV) and the Good News Bible translations (GNT) of Micah 6:8 show this: "love kindness" and "show constant love." Above all it means responding to others as sisters and brothers.

For Micah, mercy doesn't imply an emotional feeling, much less pity. Mercy, the theologian from El Salvador Jon Sobrino says, is a fundamental attitude toward the suffering of others that moves one to eradicate it out of the conviction that such suffering should not exist. He goes on to explain that this includes denouncing people and policies that cause suffering. It means unmasking lies that cover-up oppression. It urges the victims to liberate themselves from it.[1] Merciful actions are proactive to end suffering and create conditions that prevent suffering. They are actions for justice. Clearly mercy has to do with needy persons, but is more. It signals a whole way of living justly and caringly in community. Mercy and kindness are the foundations of all our relationships—human as well as with other living creatures.

Theologically, for Micah God *is* mercy and kindness. So we too are to be kind and merciful. Before God, to be good means to be kind and merciful.

Humility

When Micah says "walk humbly with God" or "live in humble fellowship with God" (6:8), he isn't referring to an attitude that takes away value from people. "Humbling" doesn't signify "humiliating" or degrading oneself. Rather, it is deep respect and obedience in recognition that no one is truly self-sufficient. Our potentialities and opportunities come from God and other people. We have, because someone else has given. For this reason, humility is gratitude. So humility as a fundamental value means to live in such a manner that gratitude is manifested in our many relationships.

---

1. Sorbino, *Principle of Mercy*, 15–26.

Ethics and Spirituality

Micah's call to "live in humble fellowship" is a warning against arrogance. When people think they are self-sufficient and lose sight of their own dependencies and frailties, they tend to think they are better than others. They suppose that their "superiority" "authorizes" them to impose on others their own programs, ideas, and even morality. They commit injustices and abuses and even think they're doing right! The capacity for self-criticism is lost. That's dangerous for convivial living. Micah synthesizes this by saying that we are to humble ourselves before God. We are to respect and obey each other with a spirit of gratitude. These are required for convivial living.

Step 2
Spirituality in Action

Practice 15

For personal reflection

1. How can Micah help you live spirituality?
2. Think about some examples of justice, mercy, and humility. How do people who show these values actually live them? How are they manifested in public or social life?

For group reflection

1. Identify a problem or current event about justice, mercy, or humility that appears in the newspaper. How are Micah's values present or absent in the problem or current event? How do you think Micah would respond? How would the group respond? What does this have to do with living spirituality?

Biblical and Spiritual Ethics

Step 3
Jesus and the Gospel Traditions

Practice 16

For personal reflection

1. In a previous "conversation," we studied the parable of the Good Samaritan. Read the parable again (Luke 10:29–37). What are the ethical and spiritual values you find in the text?
2. Thinking about the life of Jesus and the teaching of this parable, what can you learn about living spiritually?

Each of the Gospels narrates the life of Jesus in its own way. Each has its own theological reasons and historical contexts. Nevertheless, among them is agreement that compassion, commitment to the poor and needy, and love characterized his ministry. We find these same values in the parable of the Good Samaritan.

Jesus taught through parables. Luke includes many in his story of Jesus. The purpose of parables is to teach by stimulating the imagination. They don't give exact answers, but are open-ended. They help us visualize similar situations in order to find answers to our problems and situations. They help us become critically aware of how we are to live. In this sense, they are models for living spiritually.

What are some of the values found in the parable of the Good Samaritan?

I want to focus on three values that the Samaritan practices when he helps the injured person: compassion, commitment, and love. Perhaps you identified these when you read the parable. Even today these are deep values for spiritual living. Jesus's words, "Go, and do likewise" (Luke 10:37), are directed to us.

Compassion

Clearly compassion is an inseparable part of the parable. It is very similar to mercy. It signifies a relationship. Compassion involves empathy or the capacity to assume as your own the feelings, needs, and experiences of someone else. It implies commitment to the other person, so it can't be limited to pity. Solidarity is a good word to express this. This means to

Ethics and Spirituality

"stand with" the other person. True compassion motivates change or corrects whatever is hurting the other person. Because of compassion, the Samaritan took concrete measures to help the injured person.

Compassion was characteristic of Jesus. Because of his compassion, he healed the sick, taught people how to live authentically, and finally, died for their salvation. He "stood with" sinners and other needy people. The parable, like the life of Jesus, underlines compassion. Compassion is to crisscross all our relationships.

Commitment

According to the parable, the Samaritan took concrete measures to help the injured man. To act in such a manner implies commitment, that is, to deliver one's self to help another person or cause. It is to assume as one's own a responsibility or struggle that is another's. Nor is commitment abstract or general. It implies a deliberate decision, taken in favor of particular persons, groups, or causes. It is an option or preference—a "preferential option" as Latin Americans say. Our model, of course, is Jesus. He manifested an evident preference or option for the poor and dispossessed. They were the subjects of his ministry. Likewise commitment implies risk of losing something, committing errors, or even danger. When the Samaritan drew near to the injured person, he was committing himself. He made a deliberate decision. In spite of the danger of thieves, he risked helping. These values characterized the life of Jesus.

"Go, and do likewise" implies commitment. It is commitment to seek the wellbeing of others and make them part of our lives. When the Samaritan reached out to the injured, he made him his neighbor, part of his community. Real neighbors live convivially and this is the basis of community. So commitment is part of convivial life. Living spiritually means living committed to others.

Love

Recalling Charles Wesley's hymn "Love divine, all loves excelling," one of my theology professors always reminded us that God is "pure, unbounded love" and that divine love excels all other loves. No value is more important to the Christian tradition than love. It is the central theme of the Gospels and the writings of Saint Paul. Jesus is explicit: "But I say to

Biblical and Spiritual Ethics

you, Love your enemies" (Matt 5:44); "You shall love your neighbor as yourself" (Mark 12:30–31); "I am giving you these commands so that you may love one another" (John 15:17). "[T]he greatest of these is love" (1 Cor 13:13), says Saint Paul. Love is the founding value of Christian ethics and grounds spirituality.

Love is so important because "God is love" (1 John 4:8). Therefore, Christian living expresses divine love. We are to treat others as God treats us. So love is the key to truly convivial living.

In the New Testament, love is *agape* (in Greek). *Agape* is love expressed as service and commitment to others. It is selfless reaching out to care for others. In Saint Paul's "love letter" in 1 Corinthians 13:1–13, the old King James Bible uses "charity" instead of "love." Unfortunately, "charity" is often a worn-out word signifying superficial assistance. But its real meaning is quite deep. Charity implies concrete, caring actions. That's what *agape* is all about. For this reason, John Wesley always preached "love of neighbor" along with "love of God": the two go together in deep caring relationships.

Love, however, too easily is confused with sentimentalism. Sometimes it even is used as an excuse not to confront injustice. It is vital to remember that justice is integral to love. Paul Tillich explains, "Love, in the sense of *agape*, contains justice in itself as its unconditional element and as its weapon against its own sentimentalization."[2] Just as Dietrich Bonhoeffer, the German theologian murdered by the Nazis, reminded us of the difference between "cheap grace" and "costly grace," so we must remember that there is a difference between "cheap love" and "costly love." "Cheap love" is love without justice. "Costly love" puts justice in its center. It takes sides. It is conflictive. It struggles against all that stands in the way of people being able to fulfill their God-given potential. Many times these obstacles are social and political. Costly love is never easy. It can make one unpopular with some groups and persons. Costly love, just as costly grace, means total commitment.

This love is rooted in the Hebrew tradition where justice is central. So it also carries the idea of mercy, kindness, and tenderness. We saw this in Micah. The Hebrew Bible insists that love is justice, and requires concrete actions in favor of others. This is the background of the New Testament idea of love.

---

2. Tillich, *Morality and Beyond*, 39.

Ethics and Spirituality

In the New Testament, love is never an ideal. Rather it is a relationship, a way of life. It isn't possible to "have" love; love must be practiced or expressed. The Johannine writer is clear about this: "let us love, not in word or speech, but in truth and action" (1 John 3:18).

Biblical love isn't only personal. It is deeply social. That is, *agape* has social, even political, implications. Deep caring never can be limited to the individual realm. First, since love creates a new reality, it brings us together into convivial communities. Second, because deep caring is expressed through institutions and formal social and political arrangements. The person who loves struggles against poverty and social injustice. She or he advocates for laws, policies, and institutions that assure justice and community welfare. That's caring deeply!

Jesus doesn't use the word love in the parable of the Good Samaritan. He didn't have to. It's more than evident that the Samaritan expressed love. The "Go, and do likewise" is simply another way of saying "love your neighbor."

Micah 6:6–8 and Luke 10:29–37 are texts that present models of spirituality. They are ethical models because they illustrate conduct favored by God. They also summarize great biblical traditions. The values they propose are the ones that are to ground ethics as spirituality for convivial living: justice, mercy and kindness, humility, compassion, commitment, and love. These are the foundations for spiritual and biblical ethics.

Practice 17

For personal reflection

1. Many people think that compassion, commitment, and love can be lived only at the personal level. They say that in the real world of politics and economics, these values don't function. They are impractical. What do you think?
2. What are some ways to put into practice compassion, commitment, and love beyond the purely personal level?

For group reflection

1. Discuss together your personal answers.

Conversation 5

Moral Discernment and Spirituality for Convivial Living

SAINT PAUL TELLS US, "'All things are lawful,' but not all things are beneficial. 'All things are lawful,' but not all things build up" (1 Cor 10:23). What's important, Saint Paul says, is seeking the welfare of other persons. That's what "builds up."

That's easy to say. It's another thing to know exactly what to do. How do you define "beneficial" or the meaning of "build up"? What's acceptable and what isn't? In truth, the moral life isn't easy. Not just in the sense of "walking the straight and narrow." Rather, simply knowing what the "straight and narrow" is! It's not always clear what we should do in particular circumstances or relationships, especially when we didn't make the circumstances. We can see several options. None of them seem right. (Or to the contrary, they all seem right). Which do we choose? In these situations, how does one live morally?

Knowing what is "beneficial" and "builds up" is moral discernment. For Saint Paul, moral—or spiritual—life is a constant process of discerning what is beneficial and what builds up. He writes in Romans 12:2 "that you may discern what is the will of God— what is good and acceptable and perfect." Discernment is the capacity to separate and differentiate parts. It's the ability to discriminate or judge among qualities. It's knowing that not all things are equal. It's recognizing that some things are more important than others. At bottom, discernment is wisdom: a basic intuition that wells from experience, combines with reason, and moves our decisions. Spiritual guides Valerie Isenhower and Judith Todd affirm, "Discernment is appropriate anytime we have a decision to make. Large or small, the decisions of life point toward particular paths. Paying attention to the process

Ethics and Spirituality

of discerning God's desires starts us on a journey down paths that lead to abundant life."[1] So take seriously the words of Saint Paul: "test everything; hold fast to what is good" (1 Thess 5:21). Through the following steps, I will offer some guidance for moral discernment and living spiritually.

Step 1
Moral Reasoning

Practice 18

For personal reflection

1. How do you know if something is beneficial and upbuildng? What are some indications of each?
2. Are you guided by specific rules, or do you take into account circumstances?
3. Do you think consequences are important for defining moral conduct? Why?
4. How do you think other people answer these questions?

For group reflection

1. Share your personal answers with the group and discuss them together.
2. Look up "discernment" in the dictionary. What is its relevance for moral reasoning?

Discernment requires reasoning. Reason is the main (but not only), source of moral thinking. But there are different ways of thinking about ethics or morality. What really counts: rules, consequences, or circumstances?

For many people, maybe most, ethics is about following the rules. The rules themselves "contain" what is moral. So by following the rules, people will conduct themselves morally. In this way of thinking,

---

1. Isenhower and Todd, *Living into the Answers*, 16.

Moral Discernment and Spirituality for Convivial Living

consequences—good or bad—do not make an action ethical; only following the rules makes conduct moral. In this view, some things are always good. Others are always bad. Circumstances do not influence this. So some kinds of conduct are always prohibited and others always required. What counts is to be "right." In philosophy, this kind of moral understanding is called "non consequentialist" because consequences are not considered relevant. Such moral thinking is found throughout the Bible. The Ten Commandments represent this understanding of ethics. So do the many laws in Leviticus and Deuteronomy. In the New Testament, Matthew thinks this way. So do the writers of the Pastoral Epistles (Eph, 1–2 Tim, Titus). In these texts, God is experienced primarily as the giver of law. This form of moral reasoning has solid biblical and theological foundations. For people who understand ethics as following rules, obedience and judgment are emphasized as basic to the moral life. Spirituality is about living obediently in the face of judgment.

But wait minute, say a lot of other people. An action is good or bad according to its consequences. Rules are guides, but finally what counts morally is an action's effect. If it's hurtful, unfair, or destructive, then the action is bad—even if the rules were followed! Just obeying the rules can't make one's conduct ethical. You have to think about consequences and goals, this way of moral reasoning argues. Ethics is about achieving what is "good." This is called "consequentialist" morality. Means or rules are subordinated to doing what, in the end, is good. This kind of morality also is found in the Bible. The Hebrew Bible traditions of the Creation and the Promised Land are "consequentialist." So are Isaiah's and Micah's visions of the future (Isa 11:6–9; Mic 4:1–13). In the New Testament, Mark puts "consequences" before "rules" (Mark 2:23–28; 3:1–6). So does John, who calls disciples to "bear much fruit" (John 15:8). He teaches that love is the goal of all conduct. In these biblical traditions, morality is about living in such a way that these "ends" become reality. God, then, is the "horizon" always before us, calling us to go forward. Spirituality, in this line of thinking, is about orienting life toward all things good. Daily conduct leads one toward that goal.

Still another person might respond saying, "Well, rules can guide us and we have to think about consequences too. But we can't know what those mean if we don't take into account circumstances." Indeed, this person will argue that what is ethical emerges from the circumstance or "context" itself. A lot of times it isn't clear what is good. Nor does applying the rules help. That might even make things worse! So it's important to understand the circumstances or "context" and conduct oneself accordingly. Ethics, in this perspective, is not about "following rules," or "achieving good." It's about responding appropriately or doing what "fits." Ethics is being "responsible." People with this view tend to understand reality as ambiguous. It's not clear what is right or wrong, good or bad, in specific cases. Sometimes what is usually "wrong" can be "right" another time. Furthermore, times change. Finally, ethics requires one to act—even when there are no "good" choices. This is "contextual" ethics because the real situation is the key to moral action. In the Bible, we find this contextual approach especially in Saint Paul and Jesus. I noted a couple of key texts when I introduced this section. In his (authentic) writings (Rom, 1–2 Cor, Gal, Phil, and 1 Thess, Phlm), Paul's ethical advice responds to particular situations. He doesn't answer with general rules, but with advice that cares about relationships. Indeed, Saint Paul criticizes "the law" and proclaims freedom from it. For him, ethics is living in a Christ-like way. We are to "have the mind of Christ" (1 Cor 2:16). What this means is discerned in each situation. Among the Gospels, Luke draws on the Pauline tradition. This evangelist subordinates rules to human need and presents the gospel by way of many, many open-ended parables. Jesus often breaks the law because of the circumstances: the immediate needs of someone. In the tradition of Saint Paul and Luke, freedom and grace, not obedience and judgment, abound. This is because God, as freedom and grace, accompanies us as we struggle with daily living. Spirituality, then, is discerning what it means to "have the mind of Christ" as each and every day one is involved in many, many different contexts and circumstances. It is living "fittingly" or responsibly.

None of these ways of thinking about ethics is the correct way. They are all correct, but they are different. It's important to be clear about how you think about ethics. It's also important to understand that these different approaches often lead to different conclusions. So what one way might declare to be wrong, another way will say is correct. That's one reason people often disagree on what is ethical. It's important for your spirituality to be aware of how you reach ethical conclusions.

I want to add another note. These ways of reaching ethical conclusions emphasize reason. As I said, reason is fundamentally important. But it's not the only important thing. Feelings—the "heart"—also are important. The affective side of life is a source of moral understanding and conduct. How we feel about a situation influences conduct and decisions. This is because human persons aren't just "minds." We feel too. Of course we act emotionally, without thinking. That's a problem. But acting reasonably without feeling is a problem also. I believe that a person whose heart doesn't go out to those who suffer or who doesn't feel indignant before injustice is morally questionable. Moral feelings turn-on our moral brains. Ethics puts mind and heart together.

Practice 19

For personal reflection

1. Give an example of each type of moral reasoning discussed in the section. This can be from your own life, your church's teaching, the Bible, someone else.
2. Think about a moral decision you had to make. What kind of reasoning did you use? Which type of moral reasoning discussed most nearly fits the way you made your decision?

For group reflection

1. Share your answers with the group.
2. What are some advantages and disadvantages of each type of moral reasoning?
3. Which type do you think is "best"? Why?
4. What difference do your answers make?

Step 2
How to Make a Moral Decision

How does one go about analyzing an ethical problem and making a moral decision? There's no recipe to mechanically apply and presto, know what to do. The discernment process isn't always simple. It takes some thinking.

There are various factors to take into account. It's important to consider the viewpoint of different persons or groups. Sometimes something especially affects them in ways different than others. This raises the question as to who is the subject of the issue or concern. We need to think

Ethics and Spirituality

about how our own perspective or viewpoint influences our response. Then there are three moments or phases of analysis: gaining clarity as to just what is involved, interpreting the situation theologically and philosophically, and determining a particular response or course of action. I'll try to explain some of these.

Practice 20

For personal reflection

1. Study the above photograph. What stands out? Who are these people? Do they see the world as you do? Why? What is the woman thinking? What is her situation? What about the men? What does the photograph make you think about? Why? What emotions are touched? What does it say about convivial community? Could this be an ethical situation? Give the photograph a title.
2. Show the photograph to a couple of other people. Ask them the same questions. Are their answers the same? If they aren't, why?

For group reflection

1. Share your personal reflections with the group.
2. Why are there different responses to the photograph?
3. What are some factors that influence points of view?
4. Is there just one correct way to see the photograph?

Viewpoints and persons

People see ethical problems from their own viewpoint. Sex, social class, race and ethnic origin, religion, age, and other factors influence how one sees an ethical problem or question. These aren't determinative, but they're factors to be remembered. They show group tendencies, less so for individuals. This means there are diverse ideas about the same question or problem. People from lower income levels tend to evaluate economic policies differently from the captains of industry. Many times women and men respond differently to the same problem. Youth and older folk disagree on lots of matters. I well remember the Civil Rights movement of the 1960s and how whites and blacks responded very differently to racial segregation! It's important to recognize such factors when analyzing a course of moral action. They can influence your conclusions.

You also have to remember that persons are the subjects of moral interest. They should provide the logic for analysis. People are moral actors, who are also affected by decisions—their own as well as those of others. These persons function like the grammatical subject in a sentence. The subject provides the "logic" of the sentence. The ethical response is like the predicate. The predicate makes no sense without the subject. So persons are properly the focus of ethics. Of course people aren't just individuals. They are groups and categories also. This means that ethics also take into account groups and categories as moral subjects, such as "women," "Hispanics" or "African-Americans," "poor" or "rich."

This is important because the "moral subject" influences ethical analysis. This, in turn, affects moral conclusions. This is illustrated in many areas of life. For example, if the "subject"—the center and logic—of economic policies are poor people, then those policies more likely will respond to their interests. On the other hand, if the richer economic sectors are the center and logic of policies, they'll be the ones that mostly benefit. A very clear example how the "moral subject" affects the moral conclusion is abortion. If the "moral subject" is the unborn embryo, then, probably, one will oppose abortion. However if the "moral subject" is the pregnant woman, then it's possible to consider an abortion. Much of the debate about abortion really has to do with the "moral subject." Women and men often differ on abortion and other matters related to sexuality and human reproduction. The reason is obvious: men and women experience pregnancy and parenthood in very different ways. We are affected differently, hence our different conclusions. Of course there are many exceptions, but as generalizations these hold true.

Another factor in ethical analysis is whether one looks at the question from the "inside" or "outside." From the "inside" means, imaginatively, making the problem your own. It is understanding the situation from the perspective of the moral subject. From the "outside" means "it's not my problem, but here's the answer." The answers from "inside" or "outside" might be the same, but they'll probably be different. Jesus, it would seem, viewed ethical problems from the "inside." Think of the Samaritan women in John 4:1–42, the woman at the well, and John 8:1–11, the woman caught in adultery. Here Jesus demonstrates deep empathy for the women. Jesus doesn't condemn them. Rather, his responses reveal that he is "thinking like" these women—much to the consternation of the disciples and others. They saw the women only "from outside." Jesus always focused on the person, from "inside" their life situation.

Decision-making will involve three moments of analysis.

The first moment is understanding fully the question. It might seem to be something it's not. Or it might be more complicated than first thought. This moment involves using information from the social sciences, psychology, medicine and science, history, and other disciplines. This information will be helpful for knowing what's really going on. This moment depends a lot on reason and experience.

Another moment involves interpreting theologically the situation. The sociologist (and others) say such and such (first moment), but how can you reframe that in a theological way (second moment)? What do biblical and theological reflections contribute? What are some theological clues that help understand God's hopes for the situation? The Bible, ecclesial tradition, and theological reflection are basic.

Finally, the third moment is decision-making. Based on the first two moments, what course of action seems most appropriate? What best contributes to convivial living?

As I have said, there are no recipes for making an ethical decision. However looking at the question from the inside, identifying the moral subject, and following these three moments will be helpful.

Practice 21

For personal reflection

1. Apply the three moments to the following case:

    A woman friend comes over to your place because she wants to talk about a difficult decision. She is very upset and it's evident that she's been hit a few times. You've known for quite a while that her husband is abusive. He always refuses to get help. She's tired of hearing his promises to change and she is afraid for her own safety and that of their two small children. However her church teaches that divorce is immoral and that she should love and forgive her husband. It also teaches she must submit to him. She's read that in the Bible also. But her situation seems to be getting worse. She wants your support because she's decided to seek a divorce. What will you do? What advice will you give her?

2. Which of the three forms of moral reasoning—consequentialist, non consequentialist, contextualist—did you use? Why? Would your conclusion be different if you used a different form?

For group reflection

1. Share your personal response and work on the case together.

Ethics and Spirituality

Step 3
Living Responsibly

Practice 22

For personal reflection

1. Think of your many different social roles and relationships. In each, to whom are you responsible? For what are you responsible? How are you responsible? Is responsibility an ethical requirement?
2. What is the relationship between responsibility and spirituality?

Ethics as spirituality for convivial living requires responsibility. This means to live in such a way that God and others recognize that you are walking in God's pathway. In other words, "living by the Spirit." Responsibility, Dietrich Bonhoeffer explains, "is the entire response, in accord with reality, to the claim of God and my neighbor."[2] This means walking humbly with your neighbor, responding mercifully, and struggling for justice. And the place to do this is within the natural circuit of all life—*convivencia* or the *oikos* of God. "The 'world,'" Bonhoeffer continues, "is thus the *domain of concrete responsibility* that is given to us in and through Jesus Christ."[3] The criteria for evaluating whether you are doing this will be the real effects your individual and group conduct have on convivial life. This is responsible life.

The root of responsibility is "to respond." It points to the capacity to hear and answer—respond to—other persons and living creatures in the natural circuit of all life. Bonhoeffer writes, "We live by responding to the word of God addressed to us in Jesus Christ. It is a word that addresses our whole life . . . This life, lived in answer to the life of Jesus Christ . . . we call *responsibility*."[4] It is life that "answers to" God, people, and other forms of life. It's relational and contextual.

Responsibility includes two, simultaneous moments: to and for. We are responsible to someone or something, an authority or relationship to whom we are accountable. I am to be faithful and loyal to that authority or relationship. Then we are responsible for doing something as well as

2. Bonhoeffer, *Ethics*, 280.
3. Ibid., 254.
4. Ibid., 267.

for the quality of that something. Not only am I to do something, I am to do it well. I will be evaluated or "judged" accordingly. Responsibility, Bonhoeffer says, "is not merely concerned with good intention, but also with good outcome of action; not only motive, but also with content."[5]

The key is "to" because that will define "for." "To" signals God and the natural circuit of all life. The "for" points to fulfilling roles and tasks, and the consequences of our actions, or the effects of our conduct on others and the community.

The word "responsibility" isn't in the Bible. It's a modern idea. It has emerged with science, technology, transportation, mass (and instantaneous) communication, and ever-increasing horizons and alternative lifestyles. Nevertheless, we find in the Bible the same concerns that we call responsibility. The idea is rooted in God as the creative source, ground of being, and fountain of relationships; Jesus who assumed the role of servant (Phil 2:7); and the Holy Spirit who illumines our capacity to discern.

We are called to be responsible.

---

5. Ibid.

Conversation 6

Moral Imagination

THE FOLLOWING ETHICAL SITUATIONS will stimulate your moral imagination. Work on them and think and feel about how you "solve" them. Think about what might bring about joy and seriousness. Don't worry about being right, just let yourself go and do what seems best. That's what "imagination" is about. In each case, be creative and imaginative. Look for a novel approach. Think about convivial community. Don't forget that these situations may have implications beyond a personal decision. That is, they also can reflect powerful political, economic, and social interests. Try to identify some of them in your analysis. Anyway, see where your moral imagination leads you. You can do this individually or, better, with a group. Besides sitting around and sharing your ideas together, you might role play these situations. Or, divide into teams and debate them, taking different sides. Some additional propositions for debate follow. Have fun!

Step 1
Moral Situations

The Gay Youth Leader

When the president of the church's youth group came-out publically as gay, a huge scandal broke out in the church. This young man gave his life to Christ several years ago during a youth evangelism campaign. Since then he has been a positive moral example for other youth. The church has been very proud of him and pleased about his positive influence on the other young people. But now many of the longtime leaders are demanding that he be expelled from the church. Even his parents have said they don't want him in the house anymore, and some neighborhood people say he shouldn't be around them either. The young man has explained that he has no desire to cause a scandal, much less to leave the church or his home. It's just that he wants to be honest and not have to hide who he is. It's not that he wants to be gay, he says, but that he is gay. It's normal for him, so he doesn't understand why everyone wants to punish or change him. He's asked you and a number of people in the church to support him. What should the church, his parents, and the neighborhood do? Why?

Sex Education in the Middle School

Frequent teenage pregnancies are causing concern among parents and school officials. All agree that it's not just a problem of morals but also of ignorance among youth about sexuality and human reproduction. So school officials are urging that sex education be incorporated into the middle schools. The proposed curriculum includes biological information about conception, but also information about how to avoid pregnancy with contraceptives including condoms. All this has caused much controversy. Some parents say that sex education belongs only in the home. Others say it's okay in the school but not in classes with both sexes present. And others argue that nothing about contraception should be taught. This latter seems to be the real source of conflict. These people say that teaching about contraception will encourage sex among the youth. Some object that contraception is morally wrong in all situations. They say the school should teach "abstinence-only." The school argues that the curriculum doesn't take a moral position but that youth have a right to knowledge about contraception. Some supporters argue that the real concern is to prevent unwanted pregnancies and since many youth will have sex, in spite of moral prohibitions, it's preferable that they use contraception. "Abstinence-only" just doesn't work! Where do you find yourself in the debate? What position should your church take?

Thanksgiving Dinner

Thanksgiving is coming up and your church is planning a big banquet. Turkey and dressing, ham, green beans, salad, and pumpkin pie! As part of the planning committee you have to decide the menu as well as all the physical logistics, like the table arrangement, as well as the plates and eating utensils to be used. The committee wants the meal to be a time of real Christian fellowship that will reflect deep or core faith values. So how will the menu and physical arrangements symbolize these concerns? Most of the food available in grocery stores is the product of a long line of manufacturing processes based on agrochemicals, industrialized animal husbandry, and artificial ingredients. A lot of cheap labor worked in the fields and slaughterhouses to package the food and to get it to supermarkets. And what about the plates and utensils? It would be easier to use plastic plates, cups, and knives, forks, and spoons, but then, there would be an environmental cost. So, what will you suggest to the planning committee?

Life Support

Your seventeen-year-old son suffered a motorcycle accident. He's in a coma because of severe head injuries. The doctors don't believe he has any chance of recovery and probably won't come out of the coma. Even if he should, he will be severely impaired for whatever lifespan he might have. Only a respirator is keeping him alive. Within a few hours you must decide whether to continue the life support indefinitely or withdraw it and let him die. What will you do?

A Tragic Choice

Sadly, a young woman you know has given birth to conjoined twins. The baby girls are joined at their chests and share a single heart. The medical team has explained that the two will not live for long if they remain joined together. Separating them means one will die because there is only one heart. However, the heart is normally placed in the body of one of the girls. This girl, the doctors are confident, will survive and be able to mature normally. The parents are distraught. Many people including church groups are urging the operation. They want to save the baby that can survive. But many others oppose it. They argue that separation is immoral and against the will of God because it means killing a child. Even though both will die if left unseparated, they say that must be God's will because God brought them into the world conjoined. If you had to make the decision, what would it be?

Moral Imagination

Keeping Your Yard Green

Your neighborhood is proud of its well-kept, green lawns and flower gardens. You share this pride and love gardening. But keeping a top quality yard and flower garden isn't easy. Weeds are constant, insects cut down plants, and the green grass seems to fade too easily. Nevertheless, there are many garden chemicals from fertilizers to herbicides and insecticides to help you out. They do a pretty good job of keeping things green and colorful. And they are easily available at the nearby garden supply store. But they also are costly for the environment. The many chemicals wash into the streets and drainage systems, birds ingest the toxic residues, and little-by-little the chemicals sink into underlying groundwater. Beside this, the big petrochemical plants that produce them often contaminate the environment and are hazardous for workers. What do you think about this? Will your gardening be changed?

Help for Undocumented Immigrants

The state where you live is experiencing a large increase in undocumented immigrants, mainly from Mexico and Central America. They speak little or no English and work in menial jobs. They are very poor and have many needs. Your church has an outreach program for these immigrants. The church bus brings many of them to special Sunday services in Spanish, and also takes them to schools and medical services. One of your pastors is assigned to visit them in their homes. However the state alleges that they cost taxpayers millions of dollars in social services and, besides, that they are lawbreakers since they do not have legal immigration status. So a law has been passed that criminalizes hiring or giving any kind of assistance to these people. Clearly this affects your church's outreach. You remember the "Good Samaritan" and Christ's many words about caring for the poor. Yet helping these poor immigrants now is a crime. How should your church respond?

Ethics and Spirituality

Propositions for Debate

1. Marriage between persons of the same sex ought to be legal.
2. Underage or unmarried women ought to have access to contraceptives.
3. Personal use of drugs like cocaine and marijuana ought to be permitted.
4. Capital punishment ought to be prohibited.
5. Everyone ought to be allowed to carry a gun.
6. Lotteries and other forms of gambling ought to be promoted.
7. Vegetarianism ought to be a moral norm.
8. Premarital sexual relations ought to be morally permissible.
9. Plastic bags ought to be prohibited for use in grocery and other stores.
10. "Man" ought not to be used as a reference to humanity.
11. Recycling garbage ought to be required.
12. People accused of terrorism ought not to have the same rights as others.
13. Pornography and other explicitly erotic material ought to be prohibited.
14. One ought to give to beggars in the street.
15. Scientific experiments with animals ought to be prohibited.

I'm sure you can think of other propositions to debate! Feel free to do so.

Practice 23

1. Think about your answers to these questions and then discuss them with your group.
2. What are some things you learned from this exercise about how you make moral decisions?
3. What do these "moral situations" teach you about spirituality and ethics?

Bibliography

Ashley, J. Matthew. "Contemplation in the Action of Justice: Ignacio Ellacuría and Ignatian Spirituality." In *Love that Produces Hope: The Thought of Ignacio Ellacuría*, edited by Kevin F. Burke and Robert Lassale-Klein, 144–66. Collegeville, MN: Liturgical Press, 2006.
Bonhoeffer, Dietrich. *Discipleship: Dietrich Bonhoeffer Works*. Vol 4. Minneapolis: Fortress Press, 2003.
———. *Ethics: Dietrich Bonhoeffer Works*. Vol. 6. Minneapolis: Fortress Press, 1996.
Broadus, Loren. *Ethics for Real People*. St. Louis: Chalice Press, 1966.
Caputo, John D. *Philosophy and Theology*. Nashville: Abingdon Press, 2006.
Grandberg-Michelson, Wesley. *Redeeming Creation: The Rio Earth Summit—Challenges for the Churches*. Geneva: World Council of Churches, 1992.
Gutiérrez, Gustavo. *A Theology of Liberation, History, Politics and Salvation*. Maryknoll, NY: Orbis Books, 1973.
Hall, Robert T. *Moral Education: A Handbook for Teachers*. Minneapolis: Winston Press, 1979.
Hinkelammert, Franz. *El mapa del emperador. Determinismo, caos, sujeto*. San José: DEI, 1996.
Irarrázaval, Diego. *Gozar la ética*. Buenos Aires: Editorial San Pablo, 2005.
Isenhower, Valerie K., and Judith A. Todd. *Living into the Answers: A Workbook for Personal Spiritual Discernment*. Nashville: Upper Room Books, 2008.
Kaufman, Gordon D. *In the Beginning: Creativity*. Minneapolis: Fortress Press, 2004.
Kempis, Thomas à. *The Imitation of Christ by Thomas à Kempis: A New Reading of the 1441 Autograph Manuscript by William C. Creasy*. Macon: Mercer University Press, 1989.
Koll, Karla Ann. *Teología evangélica, módulo y antología de estudio*. Managua: Facultad Evangélica de Estudios Teológicos, 1994.
Lebacqz, Karen, and Joseph D. Driskill. *Ethics and Spiritual Care: A Guide for Pastors, Chaplains, and Spiritual Directors*. Nashville: Abingdon Press, 2000.
Lehmann, Paul. *Ethics in a Christian Context*. New York: Harper & Row, 1963.
Longridge, W. H. *The Spiritual Exercises of St. Ignatius of Loyola*. 5th ed. London: A. R. Mowbray, 1955.
Meyer, Robin R. *Saving Jesus from the Church: How to Stop Worshipping Christ and Start Following Jesus*. New York: HarperCollins Publishers, 2009.
Moran, Gabriel. *A Grammar of Responsibility*. New York: Crossroad, 1996.
Mudge, Lewis S. *The Church as Moral Community: Ecclesiology and Ethics in Ecumenical Debate*. New York: Continuum, 1998.
Niebuhr, H. Richard. *The Responsible Self*. New York: Harper & Row, 1963.
Pitt, Theodore. *Choose! Christian Ethics Today*. Covenant Life Curriculum. St. Louis: Christian Board of Education, 1970.

Bibliography

Schweiker, William. *Responsibility and Christian Ethics*. Cambridge: Cambridge University Press, 1995.

Sheldon, Charles M. *Morality of the Heart: A Psychology for the Christian Life*. New York: Crossroad, 1997.

Sobrino, Jon. *The Principle of Mercy: Taking the Crucified People from the Cross*. Maryknoll, NY: Orbis Books, 1994.

Tillich, Paul. *Morality and Beyond*. New York: Harper and Row, 1963.

Wesley, John. "Means of Grace." In *The Works of John Wesley*, edited by Albert C. Outler, Sermons 1, 376–97. Nashville: Abingdon Press, 1984.

www.ingramcontent.com/pod-product-compliance
Lightning Source LLC
Chambersburg PA
CBHW051714090426
42736CB00013B/2705